For Rosemary and Arthur and the spark you lit
within me to create something significant.

Marri didyarigura to Dharug Ngurra Aboriginal Corporation, and Corina Norman and Jasmine Seymour for looking over multiple drafts of *Tubowgule*, for your guidance, for your Dharug dalang lessons, and of course, for all the budyari budyari work you do to reclaim Dharug dalang for the benefit of us all.

To the Gadi people, marri didyarigura for your knowledge and presence that is felt then, now and forever. Tubowgule is rich and full with the footsteps of the ancestors leaving their mark as they continue to guide us.

MELISSA-JANE FOGARTY

For the Gadi people, whose lives, wisdom and stories breathe in every stone, river and tree of this land we call Sydney. May these pages be a small tribute to the tales that deserve to be heard, honoured and shared.

And to my niece Daisy – may you always walk this world with wonder, kindness and the courage to listen deeply.

DYLAN FINNEY

Aboriginal and Torres Strait Islander people should be aware that this book contains names and depictions of deceased persons.

TUBOWGULE

A SYDNEY OPERA HOUSE HISTORY

TUBOWGULE

A SYDNEY OPERA HOUSE HISTORY

MELISSA-JANE FOGARTY
DYLAN FINNEY

LOTHIAN Children's Books

TUBOWGULE
BEGINNING OVER 60,000 YEARS AGO ...

Where the knowledge waters meet, the Gadi people gather.
They sing, dance and voice their stories full of spirit and knowledge.

Tubowgule, pronounced **tube-uh-gahlee**, is a **Dharug** word meaning 'where the knowledge waters meet'. The meeting of waters refers to the mixing of the ocean with fresh water. This made Tubowgule a place full of resources and an important place to gather.

They fish for oysters, mussels and fish, hunt possums, wallabies and kangaroos, and pick edible plants nearby.

This place belongs to the Gadi people.

Shells and bones from the animals the Gadi people ate were left behind at Tubowgule in areas called middens. This was so that the next time people hunted or fished there they could make sure the same animals weren't taken. They only took what was needed to ensure **preservation** of the species in the area.

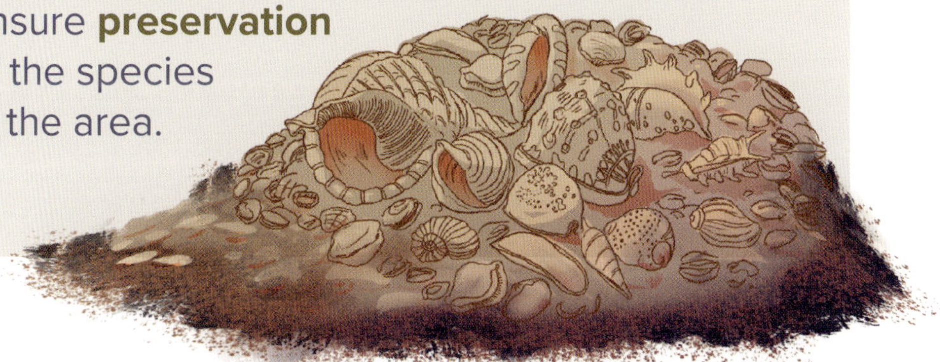

CATTLE POINT

1788, APPROXIMATELY 250 YEARS AGO ...

The British arrive on the First Fleet, led by Governor Arthur Phillip.
With the boats and the people come cattle and horses.
Tubowgule is claimed by the British colonisers to house the
new beasts, and they roam their fenced space with no place to escape.

Though the British colonisers claimed the land, Aboriginal people still frequented the area, with women heard singing while they fished and ceremonies taking place during the night that featured **dancing and singing**.

LIMEBURNERS' POINT

1788, APPROXIMATELY 250 YEARS AGO ...

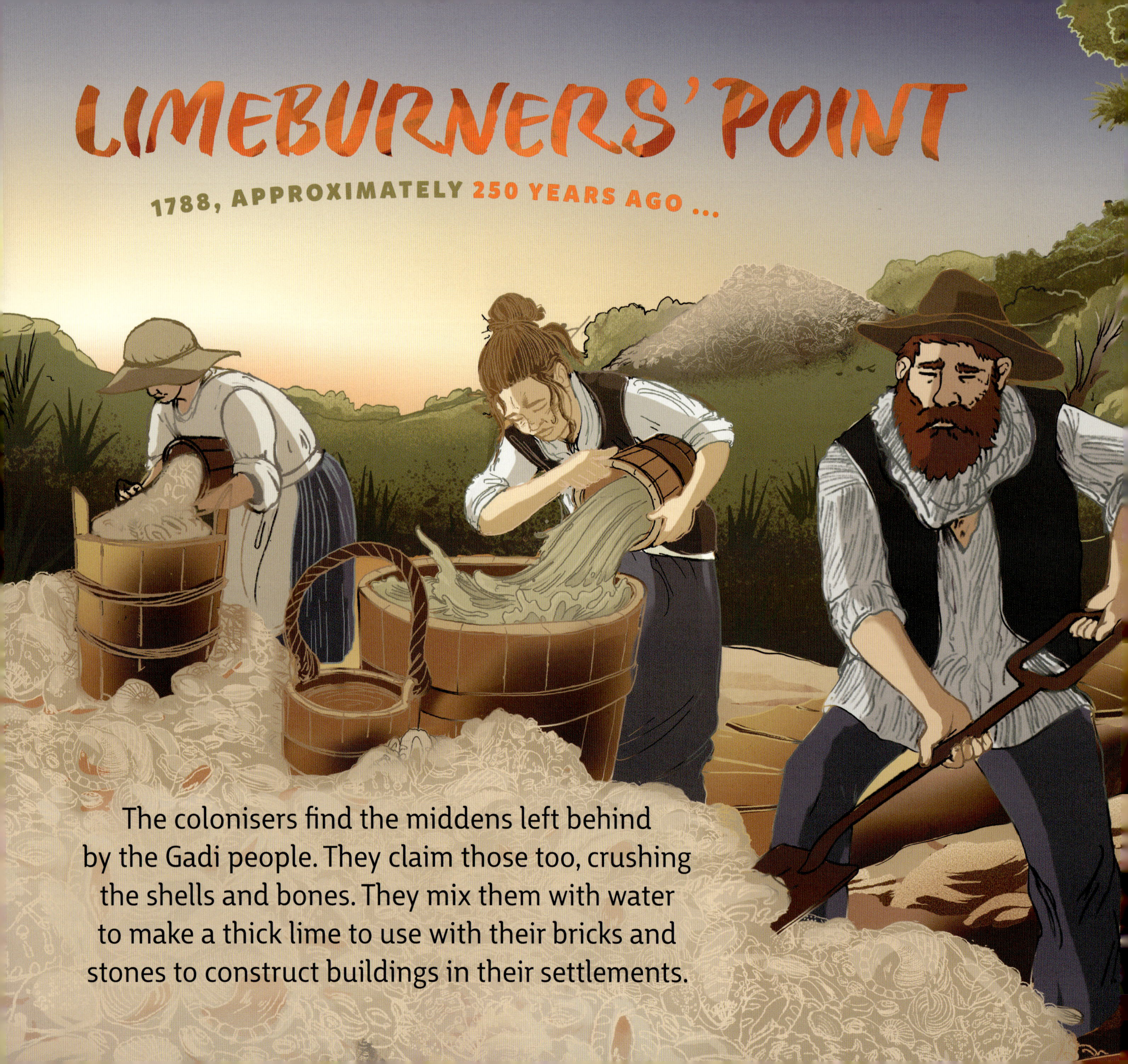

The colonisers find the middens left behind by the Gadi people. They claim those too, crushing the shells and bones. They mix them with water to make a thick lime to use with their bricks and stones to construct buildings in their settlements.

Convict women gathered the shells and bones and burnt them to create lime **mortar**.

There was only one building constructed from the **lime** from Limeburners' Point: Government House on Bridge Street.

BENNELONG POINT
1790, APPROXIMATELY 250 YEARS AGO ...

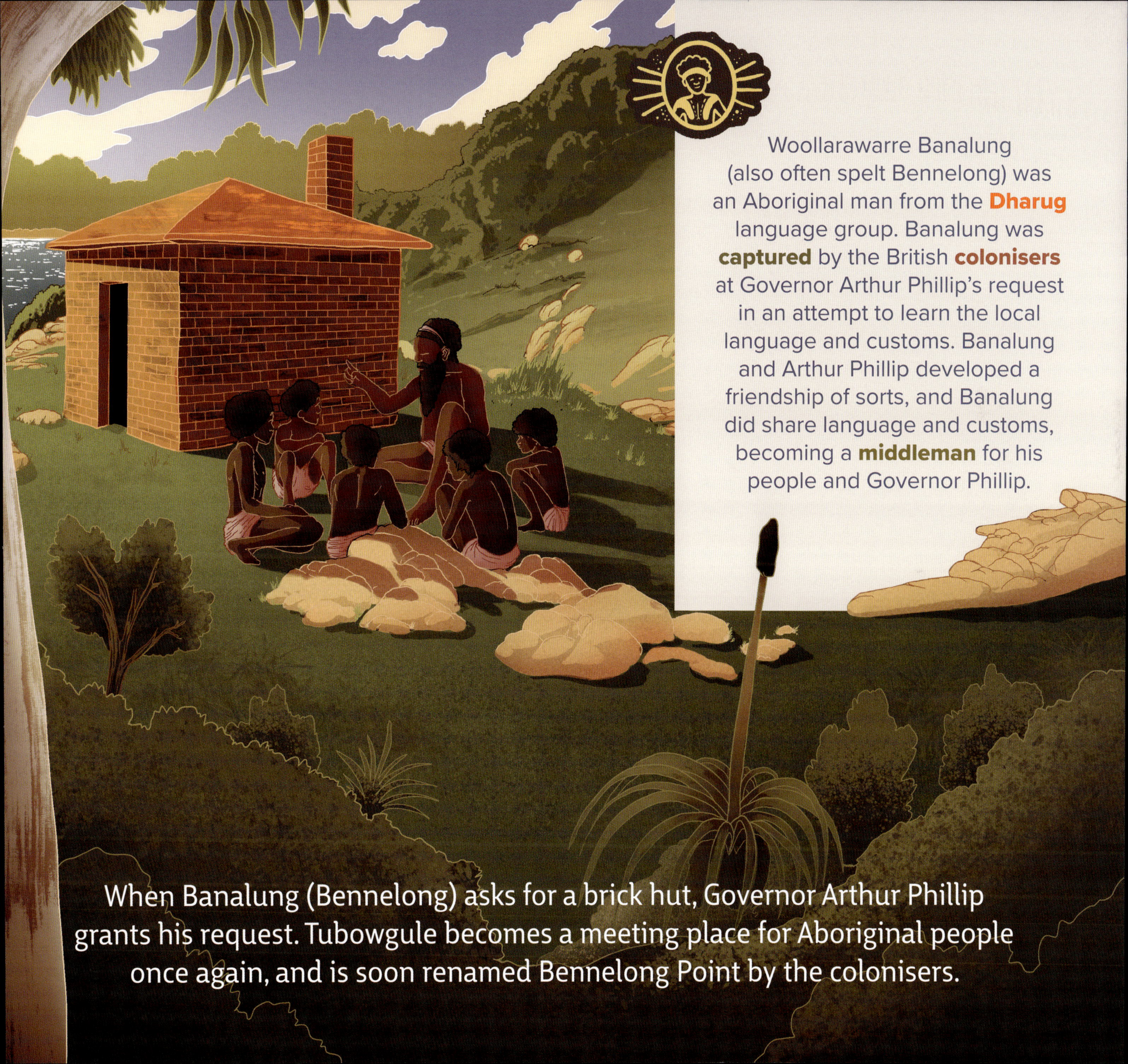

Woollarawarre Banalung (also often spelt Bennelong) was an Aboriginal man from the **Dharug** language group. Banalung was **captured** by the British **colonisers** at Governor Arthur Phillip's request in an attempt to learn the local language and customs. Banalung and Arthur Phillip developed a friendship of sorts, and Banalung did share language and customs, becoming a **middleman** for his people and Governor Phillip.

When Banalung (Bennelong) asks for a brick hut, Governor Arthur Phillip grants his request. Tubowgule becomes a meeting place for Aboriginal people once again, and is soon renamed Bennelong Point by the colonisers.

Banalung's hut is torn down not long after he returns from a three-year trip to London.

Banalung was the **first Aboriginal man** to visit and return from **Britain**. Along with his friend, Yemmerrawanne, Banalung accompanied Governor Phillip on a trip where the Aboriginal men were kept busy with activities such as going to the theatre and attending parliament. Yemmerrawanne fell ill and died while in Britain and Banalung became homesick, though it was another two years before he made it home.

Banalung instead settles at Kissing Point with his wife, Boorong.

FORT MACQUARIE

1817, APPROXIMATELY 210 YEARS AGO ...

What was once a gathering place becomes a fort that houses men and weapons. While the fort is being built, the channel separating the point from the mainland is filled with rocks. Tubowgule and the mainland are now connected.

The stone fort is a square with three of its sides facing the water, making it easy to see enemies approaching. In the middle, there's a tower with a guardroom and storehouse, and underneath there are barrels of gunpowder. There's enough space for one officer and eighteen men.

Ex-convict and architect **Francis Greenway** was ordered by Governor Lachlan Macquarie to construct the fort. The fort was designed in an ancient style and described as **strange** and **whimsical** – it even had a drawbridge! Greenway also designed St James' Church, Government House and Hyde Park Barracks in Sydney. Fort Macquarie existed for eighty years but was demolished in 1901 as it wasn't being used anymore.

FORT MACQUARIE TRAM SHED

1902, APPROXIMATELY
120 YEARS AGO ...

When the fort is demolished, the Fort Macquarie Tram Shed is built. The shed is designed to look like a fortress in honour of the fort that stood before it. The depot has twelve tracks and a twelve-road shed with a loop line around the outside.

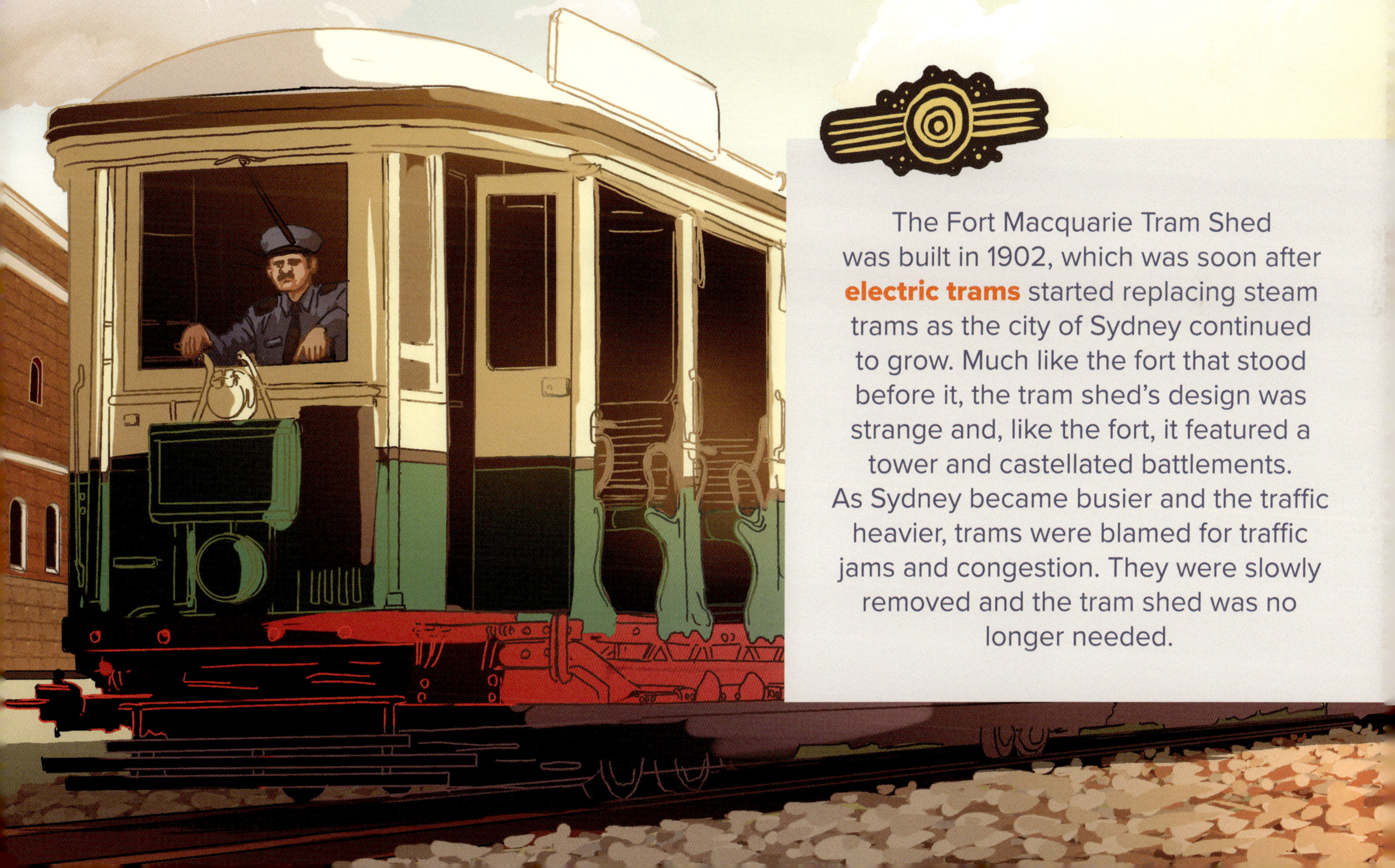

The Fort Macquarie Tram Shed was built in 1902, which was soon after **electric trams** started replacing steam trams as the city of Sydney continued to grow. Much like the fort that stood before it, the tram shed's design was strange and, like the fort, it featured a tower and castellated battlements. As Sydney became busier and the traffic heavier, trams were blamed for traffic jams and congestion. They were slowly removed and the tram shed was no longer needed.

SYDNEY OPERA HOUSE

1955, APPROXIMATELY 70 YEARS AGO ...

Tubowgule, now known as Bennelong Point, is chosen as the site for a state-of-the-art venue for opera, ballet, theatre and a variety of performances from around the world. A competition for the design of the venue is launched with 233 entries submitted from architects worldwide.

Sydney Harbour was now a well-known place around the world and the government believed it was in need of a **new concert hall** that would further modernise the city. **Eugene Goossens,** the director of the NSW Conservatorium of Music, had been calling for a new concert hall for more than a decade, and suggested Bennelong Point as the location.

With his unique and controversial design, Jørn Utzon from Denmark is declared the winner of the design competition.

Jørn Utzon's design submission was numbered 218, and it's been said that his entry was pulled from an already-rejected pile by one of the four judges, Eero Saarinen, who declared that it was easily the winner.

‘We have returned again and again to the study of these drawings and are convinced that they present a concept of an Opera House which is capable of becoming one of the great buildings of the world,’ the competition judges write. ‘Because of its very originality, it is clearly a controversial design. We are however, absolutely convinced of its merits.’

Construction on the Opera House begins on 2 March 1959. It is not officially opened until 20 October 1973. The long-awaited opening is a grand affair with helicopters flying over and marching bands, military personnel and dignitaries from surrounding countries completing a procession.

There were many problems during construction, including the difficulty in constructing the sails, a huge increase in the cost and Jørn Utzon leaving, but Australian architect **Peter Hall** was able to pull it all together and complete the project.

Queen Elizabeth II officially opens the Sydney Opera House: 'The Sydney Opera House has captured the imagination of the world, though I understand that its construction has not been totally without problems. The human spirit must sometimes take wings or sails, and create something that is not just utilitarian or commonplace.'

WORLD HERITAGE

In 2007, the Sydney Opera House was added to the **UNESCO World Heritage List** because of its unique and daring design and construction that has influenced modern architecture. Being a World Heritage-listed site means that the Sydney Opera House will be protected and preserved for future generations.

I AM BANALUNG, AND MY SPIRIT, AND THE SPIRIT OF MY PEOPLE LIVES. AND THEIR DANCE, THEIR MUSIC AND THEIR DRAMA AND THEIR LAUGHTER ALSO REMAINS.

Aboriginal actor and descendant of Banalung, Ben Blakeney, perches atop the highest sail of the Opera House and officially welcomes people to the site as his ancestor.

The Sydney Opera House is now an Australian icon and one of the most-recognised buildings in Australia and the world.

Though Tubowgule was taken from the Gadi people, it is once again a place of gathering where songs are sung, stories are told, dances are danced and knowledge and culture are shared.

Aboriginal and Torres Strait Islander **performances** are an important feature at the Opera House today, along with all kinds of events including comedy shows, ballet performances, musical acts and more, showcasing entertainers from all around the world.

Tubowgule was an important place for Aboriginal people due to its richness of resources. The mixing of fresh water and salt water, also known as an estuary, is a place where many aquatic species breed and thrive, which attracts other wildlife to the area. With such an abundance of life, it was an important area for fishing, hunting, gathering and ceremony.

Early coloniser Governor John Hunter reported hearing Aboriginal women singing on Tubowgule while fishing, and another, General Watkin Tench, saw Aboriginal women bodysurfing in the waters from Milson's Point to Tubowgule.

There was also white clay called dabuwa at the point, which would have been used as body paint for ceremonies. There were often garabara, or corroborees, at night where many clans would come together to sing and dance. This would have been lots of fun, but these gatherings were also a way of storytelling and passing on knowledge about Country.

When the colonisers arrived, they thought Tubowgule was a good place to fence in their cattle, and they also realised that the build-up of shells and bones, called middens, left by Aboriginal people over many thousands of years, could be crushed and used to make mortar for new buildings.

The colonisers didn't understand the significance of the land or the middens that displayed a vast history of the people who frequented the area. The middens let the Aboriginal people know what had been eaten previously and what they should hunt to stop destruction of species.

Though the British used Tubowgule for their own purposes, in 1790 a hut was built there for Banalung, and it was here that Banalung and friends held a garabara for the colonisers in 1792. Aboriginal people frequented Tubowgule once again, and it soon became known as Bennelong Point.

Banalung's hut didn't stand for long. It was torn down soon after he returned from a trip to London. Banalung settled at Kissing Point instead of Bennelong Point.

Around twenty years later, during the construction of Fort Macquarie on Bennelong Point, the channel was filled with rocks taken from the point, which changed the formation of Tubowgule forever.

Despite the changes that have occurred at Tubowgule, the significance of the place lives on. Queen Elizabeth II opened the Sydney Opera House in 1973, but it was Banalung's descendant Ben Blakeney who officially welcomed visitors to the House.

Since the opening, Aboriginal performances have been a feature of the Opera House, but even more so since 2012 when the First Nations program was launched. The program ensures that Aboriginal culture and performances are still deeply intertwined with and integral to the Sydney Opera House.

Tubowgule has changed significantly over the years but it remains a place of gathering: to dance, sing and perform, and continue the traditions of the oldest living culture in the world.

Note on language from the author: There can be variations on spelling and pronunciation of language, and though I have done my best in this book with the knowledge I have, any errors are my own.

A Lothian Children's Book
Published in Australia and New Zealand in 2025
by Hachette Australia
Gadigal Country, Level 17, 207 Kent Street, Sydney, NSW 2000
www.hachettechildrens.com.au

Hachette Australia acknowledges and pays our respects to the past, present and future Traditional Owners and Custodians of Country throughout Australia and recognises the continuation of cultural, spiritual and educational practices of Aboriginal and Torres Strait Islander peoples. Our head office is located on the lands of the Gadigal people of the Eora Nation.

NATIONAL LIBRARY OF AUSTRALIA
A catalogue record for this book is available from the National Library of Australia

ISBN: 978 0 7344 2335 1 (hardback)

Cover and internals designed by Liz Seymour
Colour reproduction by Splitting Image
Printed in China by 1010 Printing International Limited